Of Things To Come

by Myrtle Stedman

SUNSTONE
PRESS

SANTA FE

Cover Art by Myrtle Stedman

Sunstone books may be purchased for educational, business, or sales promotional use.
For information please write: Special Markets Department, Sunstone Press, P.O. Box 2321,
Santa Fe, New Mexico 87504-2321.

FIRST EDITION

Library of Congress Cataloging in Publication Data:
Stedman, Myrtle.
Of things to come/by Myrtle Stedman. —1st ed.
p. cm.
Poems.
ISBN: 0-86534-274-1
I. Title.
PS3569. T33823045   1998
811' .54—dc21   98-10978
CIP

Published by SUNSTONE PRESS
Post Office Box 2321
Santa Fe, NM 87504-2321 / USA
(505) 988-4418 / *orders only* (800) 243-5644
FAX (505) 988-1025

Dedicated to the Director of the Fine Arts Museum of New Mexico, Stuart Ashman, with whom I have had a long and fruitful association.

CONTENTS

Chapter I

OF THINGS TO COME

OF THINGS TO COME

I am a babe
   a lover
      and an old woman

I am a painter
   an architect of adobe structures
      a writer

and what they honor in Santa Fe as
   a "Living Treasure"

Scientists and astrophysicists have yet to find another planet having life and culture on it; yet around five billion years ago life began on this planet in forms which could make copies of themselves. The scientists say that the forms knew how to do it.

    When asked, "how did they know how to make copies of themselves?" the scientists replied that it would take an artist or a poet to tell us that.

How about this piece of poetry—

In the beginning was the Word,
   and the Word was with God,
      and the Word was God.

The same was in the beginning
   with God.

All things were made by him;
   and without him was
      not anything made
         that was made.

In him was life; and the
   life was the light of
      men.

And the light shineth in

darkness; and the
   darkness comprehended
      it not.
         —St. John, 1:1-5

And this—

And by his Word:
   ...Let us make man
      in our image,
         after our likeness...

...So God created man
   in his *own* image...

...Male and female
   created he them.
      —Genesis, 1:26-27

The astrophysicists have a mind-boggling knowledge of the cosmos but they find no God or gods out there in the heavens. And they find that all life is of the same "stuff" as the universe. The vast variables are in the way we are put together and in our behavior.

So back to the poem we have just read to see if we find truth in poetic form, or the knowing that was in the beginning that made life in the male and female model as created.

The scientists don't agree on the question—was the universe created—but if not, we certainly are driven by a creative mind, and see no end to creative potentiality.

This creativity we share with everything in the universe, down to the nuts and bolts of everyday life as male and female, which should be scientific proof that mentality is the universal drive, or life, of the universe.

I want to share a poem I wrote in 1947, which came to me in my dire need to know how the mind works:

Imagine if you can an infinite death-like before-time rest—
Virgin mind in semiconscious repose.
Close your eyes and all is darkness, as far as you can see.
Watch, for there is a quickening and a flickering of light to be observed.
Then rest again while you contemplate what you have seen.
But look, for the darkness quickens again and again in a chain that
    becomes a necessity for the light to possess her and she him.
And where she draws him, she also follows;
So that there is a breathing increasing until it mounts into an agonizing
    stillness, then there is a blinding flash and an explosive declaration
    in the giving and the taking.
After the recession and when there is again a period of rest, and change
    can be observed, there is light and darkness, divided yet one.
And the darkness is pregnant with form.

Except for the darkness longing for the light of mind there would be no beings visible in form, nor any tangible ideas separated from the intangible. Light is the brilliance of mind—darkness gives it shape and form.

If all were light we could see nothing. If all were darkness we could see nothing. With the two together we can see and understand what we see. So it should not be said anymore—

And the light shineth in darkness
And the darkness comprehended it not.

We have evolved from the "explosive declaration," or the "Big Bang" if you will, for over fifteen billion years. Until the scientists prove otherwise, we are unique in the universe.

If the cultured of the planet begin to appreciate each others' cultures *as* cultures, and *not* absolute truths, we have a chance of surviving a few more billion years.

To see God as mind
   is not to belittle God
      but to see how
         great God is—

As a universal presence
   of mind yet to be
      understood.

Not just in an egghead
   somewhere out there
      but

The very stuff we
   and everything,
      animate and inanimate,

Are made of.

So the basic thing to understand
   about life and its endeavors

Is that the mind is
   male and female

In that it is expressive
   and receptive

Thus biological.

The spiritual connotation
   comes from the
      attitude or urge
         to do it.

Whatever "it" is.

Vast or great civilizations
   have been destroyed—

Species extinguished
   and new ones
      appear.

We can think of God
   as an artist or a poet

With a pencil in one hand
   and an eraser in the
      other.

So that the word
   may be clear
      in the poem

And the art be
   apparent in
      the art work;

The reverberation of
   the Big Bang if you
      will, or the spirit in
         the explosive declaration

To do it
   in everything
      in the universe.

OF ONE MIND

If all is of one mind,
    and that mind
        perfection in itself,

How do we account
    for sickness
        and atrocities?

"The darkness
    comprehended
        it not"

I find nothing
    wrong with
        the darkness,

It is the receptive
    side of the
        mind.

It is the other half
    of the whole.
The half that
    gives birth
        to consciousness.

But children
    have to be taught
        and told.

That is where the
    problem
        lies—

And that, not in the
    children

They are born
    perfect

With ten fingers
    and toes,

But there is so much
    they or we have
        to learn

Before we come
    anywhere
        near

The perfection of consciousness
    which is our birthright
        to know,

That we are of one mind.

One by one we become
    conscious
        of this fact

And want to tell
    the whole
        world.

There is not a Divine
    Mind

And a human
    mind

There is just
    mind,

In everything everywhere.

Our consciousness
        soars to
                divine
                        heights

Or dips to depths
        of degradation.

The latter being
        self-evident

So it is time that
        we shape
                up—

And know,
        that the mind
                is everywhere
                        in the universe.

Our consciousness
        is like a flashlight
                in our hand,

Lighting up a single
        area at a time,

Where it is directed.

"FATHER GLORIFY THOU ME

That I might
    glorify thee,"

Is the greatest
    petition made
       by man.

But when we know
    that "thee and
       me"

Is the same
    it will be
       greater
         still.

Keeping this knowledge
    secret—except
       for adepts—and
         the church

Will not be permissible
    anymore.

This secret has been
    the culprit
       all along.

If we truly know
    the meaning
       of this

There would be no
    need for
       misuse.

This is a big order
    that needs to be
       turned over

To the universal
    mind.

It really hasn't been
    a secret

We have just misread
    the signs.

Chapter II

THE UNIVERSAL MIND

THERE ARE DOCUMENTED

Cases of two or three
   women living
      without taking
         food

There is one well-known
   for bleeding when
      thinking of the
         Christ;

What do they prove?

They prove only
   a strong dedication
      of mind

And what it can
   do in extreme
      cases.

Sensibly or no.

There are those
   who hear and
      talk to the
         dead.

It is the same
   thing.

The mind is absolutely
   fantastic.

There is nothing
   it cannot
      do.

It is certainly time
   to be aware
      of this.

It should no longer
   be left up to
      the few.

It has been only
   the few who
      have been
         controlling

This mess that
   we are in.

In bombings and
   shootings and
      thefts.

Poverty is not just
   in empty pockets,

It is in a lack of
   knowledge

Of how the mind
   works.

It's not a lack
   of ability—

We have plenty
   of that.

There is nothing
a man cannot
do

Under directed
insight.

What insight will
take us to

The things to
come?

THE UNIVERSAL MIND

Is male and female

If I ask, "where is a
     thing?"

My hand can reach
     out and touch
          it.

If I am driving fast
     and a voice
          says to me,
               "slow down,"

I slow down.

This kept me, one dark
     stormy night,

From driving right into
     the path of dark
          horses dashing
               across the
                    road.

This tells me that
     the mind is out
          there conscious

Of me and all of
     my surrounding
          consequences.

One part of the universal
     mind knows

The other part
     receives the knowledge
          and turns it into
               consciousness.

This happens
     not just out
          there

There is not a spot
     where it is not
          knowing and
               understanding.

The more we are
     aware of this,

The more the mind
     serves us—

On a universal
     scale.

WHEN THE CREATOR SAID

Let us make man
    in our image

This was an intercourse
    between itself
        and its counterpart.

We hear but don't see
    until the image
      is made

But the image is the
    image of an expressive
      and receptive
        mind.

When we ask, "What image
    do you have of
      yourself?"

We are not asking for
    a portrait.

We are asking, "how do
    you feel about
      yourself?"

Or, "how do you want
    others to think
      of you?"

And the way they think
    of you is the way
      they see

And understand you.

The outward appearance
    of this is the male
    and female

You can't have
    one without
    the other.

AND IS THE FATHER IN

Heaven all righteousness;
  not a father
    that can be
      brutal or
        mean?

It is totally impersonal—
  it just lets us
    alone

To, on our own,
  become conscious
    of what he
      is

Through our own
  observation.

He can't help but
  love

That is his business

We just call it love.

The Big Bang
  banged and

The wave waves
  still and there is
    a gentle reaction

That holds and
  mothers that
    love

And bears a consciousness
  in the image

Of wave interacting with
  wave—

In the image of that
  love;

Having all of its creative
  potential

And all of the memory
  of what has
    been done

Hidden in rock
  and bone,

And atom

To be found later on
  little by little

Until we are fully
  grown.

THE MIND IS REPRODUCTIVE

It creates its own kind.

And, that goes forth
    and creates its
        own kind.

There are generations
    and generations
        of the mind.

There are sons and
    daughters of
        the mind,

Each generation is getting
    smarter and smarter

Or stupider and stupider.

All are born of this mind

Consciousness is only
    that which is born
        of the mind.

Consciousness is a babe

And always will be a babe,

Or I should say
    a child of the
        mind

No matter how old
    it becomes,

Or how many children
    it produces.

Consciousness could
    produce nothing
        if it were not

Inherently mind,
    half-baked or
        otherwise.

Mind works on a
    sliding scale,

Octave by octave,
    up or down.

For "Lo! I am the
    beginning and
        the ending."

THE UNIVERSAL MIND

Is ours to live
    by

Or die.

It is pure potential.

It is said, "If ye know
    both good and
        evil

Ye shall surely die."

Though we die

The mind remains
    the pure potential

And will make us again
    to live

And love.

AT LAST

We can no longer
    have clans or
        small groups
            of people.

With rigid rules
    which separate
        us from other
        people.

Communication
    is fluid

There are no secrets
    any more
        in a universal
        mind.

All wars have been
    between factions
        that disagree
            with one another.

The world is not
    for small
        people
            anymore.

It is all or none,
    now.

The universal mind,

The Creator
    has brought
        us to itself
        at last.

And how did it
    do it?

It did it and
    will do it

By working within
    all of us.

Because we are
    what the
        mind is.

HAVE YOU THE EARS

To hear unspoken
    truth

Or maybe it is in
    words,

But spoken in
    silence?

Then you are not
    sick—

Or you could be,

But ask the mind;

You are talking to it

And with it
    all the time.

I HAVE JUST REALIZED

That the mind
    is the hologram—
        the wholeness

We have attempted
    to find in ourselves—

While it has been
    there all of
        this time.

On this earth we
    have had a
        chance to

Discover each part
    of the whole
        as male or
            female—

As expressive or
    receptive

As light and darkness
    which gave us
        only the image
            we could
                see.

The image is a picture
    of the hologram.

We have seen the whole
    in individuals
        and things.

Or had a chance,
    that is to see.

I see that this is
    what the world
        is coming to
            now.

"I AM, THAT I AM"

The form and life
    of all that is
        or can be

I make myself
    in my own
        image

Of what I wish to be,
    for I am not alone

There is a shadow
    side of me

Without it I could
    not take
        form

It bears my name
    and bears my
        form

Yet can be and is
    as invisible
        as I mostly
            am.

Without my shadow
    I am Light

But I am not alone
    or you would
        not be.

Life is the interplay
    between my shadow
        and me.

HOW CAN WE POSSIBLY

Question planetary
    order

When even chaos comes
    in an orderly
        fashion.

The astronomers and
    the weatherman
        make their predictions
        days and centuries
            ahead.

The simplest biological
    plant comes
        and goes

Accordingly.

I always loved the
    line in the Bible
        that goes,

"Lord, I believe—
    help thou my
        unbelief."

There are kings and lords,
    barons and
        heads of state

But let us get down
    to the bottom
        of the barrel
            and ask

Who are we?

A rotten apple?

I also have always
    loved the line,

"If you make your
    bed in hell,

There am I also."

The greatest order
    proceeds without
        any restrictions;

And places itself
    anywhere and everywhere,
        without question.

WHAT HAVE I GOT ON MY MIND TO DO?

Nothing has been happening.

   Why?

I have planned and
   imagined too.

But nothing is happening.

   Why?

Have I wished too hard?

Have I played God?

Have I pushed too far?

Does fear that I won't
   get what I want
      stand in my
         way?

WHEN I AWAKE IN THE MORNING SOMETIMES

I feel anger.

I blame it on the atmosphere
   surrounding the
      whole world.

I pull the blanket over
   my head, turn
      over and try
        to go back
           to sleep.

I can't—I am on
   my back staring
      at the cracks
        and knots

In the boards above
   my head.

The anger is in me;

I put myself out—

Did far more for
    someone than
        I should have,
            moneywise,

Expecting them
    not just to thank
        me for my
            hospitality,

But to ask, "How much
    did all this cost
        and what can

We give toward
    what you did
        for us?"

Why did I put myself
    out

Why not do the simple
    thing, which
        would have cost
            nobody anything?

Are we, nationwide,
    an overgenerous
        people

Doing things we cannot
    afford,

Putting it all on a
    credit card

Hoping a sweepstakes
    will pay
        out?

I did what I did
    because I wanted
        to—

Why can't I settle
    for that?

What I did was like
    a painting.

I don't paint to sell.
    If someone wants to
        buy it I am
            pleased,

But I didn't do it
    for that.

What am I getting
    at?

Has anything moved
    in my brain?

PRESENT DAY REALITIES

Have always been
    falling apart

To be replaced by new
    realities

But never so many
    or so fast
        as the present

Which has always
    been true.

Memory is the thing
    that gives way
        by permission,

Or holds fast.

We knowingly
    or unknowingly
        make the
            choice.

When we make up
    our minds for change,

That automatically
    changes the
        reality.

We have been doing
    this ever since
        the world began.

HOW CAN THE THOUGHTS

That I have had
   this morning
     be put into
       words?

I woke with a sense
   of disconnection

Which turned quickly
   into one of
     attachment.

This is the freedom
   we long for,

This is the freedom
   found in the
     mind—

The freedom of
   attachment
    and the
      freedom to
       let go.

This is the way
   the mind
    works.

It hurts to be stuck
   in one position
    or another.

The hurt tells us
   to go for it
    or
     to let go.

I cried until I saw
   the beauty
    in this.

Now, I am laughing
   with the tears
    still in my
    eyes.

LET US CONSIDER

All wrongs as
    dung,

And plow them under
    to enrich our
        ground.

LET US FORGET

The fairy tales
    we have read
        or heard and
            taught our children.

Let us forget the
    lives we have
        lived

And live
    atop them
        all.

SAVING GRACE

We have judged,
    been judged,
        felt guilty
        and disgraced.

All this can be wiped
    away in
        minutes.

We have filled the
    atmosphere
        with hate

Our home may vibrate
    in fear and
        waste.

All this can be wiped
    away in
        minutes

By activating a single
    principle,

Within our memory,
    that mind expresses
        and conceives
            itself as it wants
                to be,

And that by knowing that, that is
    all there
        is to being.

IT WAS AND IS

I know that it is true
    that I can think,
        of he who is long gone
    from here, yet a part of
    me.

And in my mind
    right all the
        wrongs

By blessing them for what
    they told me

And see our relationship
    as pure as "Love Divine"

For surely it was
    and is
        divine.

Because it suited me,
    and suits me,
        still.

WHERE THE POTENTIAL IS

I want to see
    and I want
        to hear

With the mind
    that is all
        seeing

And all hearing.

That is not an
    impossible
        dream.

Because that is the
    only mind
        there
           is.

Within it
    is my
        potential.

I AM AND YOU ARE

Individual offshoots
   of the universal
      mind.

If we were not
   we would not
      be conscious.

But since the mind
   is universal
      there is no
         loss—

No loss of consciousness.

The mind of necessity
   is always
      conscious
         of itself

Universally and
   individually—

In the smallest
   there is the
      greatest—

A paradigm
   this is
      called.

To recognize the
   greatest in the
      smallest

Is the only way
   to get
      along.

If we do not
   recognize
      this

We are at war.

Luckily harmony
   is always a
      potential.

A probability
   for us all.

This is an eventual
   must

For it is the midstream
      that in a flood
         sweeps clear
            the shallows,

And rights itself.

"BEFORE THEY CALL,

I will answer.

While they are yet
    speaking
        I will hear."

Why?

Because—

The mind that says "I"
    is the mind that
        is in you
            and me

And is mindful of
    everything
        everywhere.

Chapter III

WHAT DO THE SCIENTISTS MEAN

WHAT DO THE SCIENTISTS MEAN

By "a unified field?"

They mean just that—
   no breaks,
      no blocks,
         no resistance,
      no time,
         no space,
      no distance.

They are talking about
   that which is—

Not about that which
   is not.

They are talking about
   mind.

They are talking about
   the "non-stuff
      of all stuff."

They are talking about
   the unity that
      exists in
         creativity,

Meaning between the
   expressiveness
      and receptivity
         of the mind.

A joint activity—

The spirit in which
   all is made
      or unmade—

By joint intent—

Unified love
   of what two phases
   of the mind
      are doing
   together—

Call it God,
Call it Spirit,
Call it Love,

The vapor of
   all solid
      things—

OUR DESIRES

Are like holes
    in the ground
      before a
        rain,

And the rain comes,
    when there is
      no objection
        to rain.

THE MIND'S SAFETY VALVE

Destruction is the mind's
    safety valve

Destruction destroys
    itself

And transforms
    that which was
        destroyed.

It is the good that
    is caught up
        in the destruction

That is the saving grace
    of a destructive
        act.

The creative mind
    saves the idea
        if it is good
           and gives it
      a better
        image.

If there is rebellion
    over atrocities
        that is the good
           in the atrocity.

The good will
    survive.

It survives in the transformation.

This is what we
    should clamp
        our thoughts
        upon.

This alone will silence
    our grief—

The knowledge that
    the mind—

The Creator is good—
    or we would
        not even be
        here

In the first place.

WHAT DID CHRIST SAY

"Father, the hour is come;
     glorify thy Son
          that thy Son also
               may glorify
                    thee."
               —John 17:1

What father was he
     talking to?

Because he didn't
     know an
          earthly
               father,

Of his own

He was able to put
     his finger
          on the

Father of all fathers and sons;

On the meaning
     of father

The creator in all—

The biological urge—

The inspirational one,

The inventor,

The investigator,

The navigator,

The map maker,

The Nobel Prize winner,

The lover,

The life,

The energy,

The will to be
     all that a
          father is;

And "is"
     is to say exists—

In forms we
     can feel
          and touch,

Or in non-form
     that we can
          understand.

It is time that
     the women in us

Stop throwing to the
     winds

All reason
     when we love

And ask
 what have we
  mothered
   and why?

Not why do we
 love—

That goes without
 saying.

Have we loved just
 to satisfy the
  biological
   urge,

Have we loved
 to hate,

To take revenge,

To have our own
 way,

To remain stubbornly
 in worn out
  ways,

In beliefs
 which have no
  basic foundation,

What are we
 mothering?

It is time we women—
 as women—
  should ask;

Not someone
 in cloth
  decorated in
   gold

Or wearing a badge
 of honor
  on his chest,

But ask ourselves,
 not our mothers before
  us either

(Though we may bless
 their souls);

But look upon everyone,
 everything and
  especially
   ourselves

With compassion
 and ask

What are we mothering?

We of all people
 should
  know.

For we are blessed
 with the thing
  a man alone
   can't do—

We are as heavenly
 as anything can
  come.

It is time for us to
    get down to
        earth

And take that heavenly
    thing into everything
        we give life to—

Both women and
    men

And promote respect
    for that which
        a man loves
            most

Which is women
    simply because
        they are men,

Homemakers,
    And fathers and sons.

Or we might ask—

Do they love us,
    or are we just
        a tool

In their kit of
    tools?

And do we love
    them?

Of course we
    do.

I HAVE NO PROBLEM

With calling mind
    God

I love to call it
    God

I have no problem
    with calling God,

"Our Father who art
    in heaven."

Are we not all in
    heaven

On a planet?

And God, the father
    of all invention

But mother too,
    to make all
        so—

And make the inventor
    father?

There would be
    no father
        but for her.

So let us get it
    straight.

The mind is male
    and female.

We have no problem
    with male and
        female

In talking about
    electricity,

Or nuts and bolts;

So why have
    a problem

With the most important
    male and female
        of them all?

Or about the
    male and
        female

Being heavenly
    wherever they
        are?

And due
    all respect,

And not
    a game, but
        pleasant

As all heavenly
    things

Are considered
    to be.

THE TIME FOR RECOLLECTION

God is my man,
   and man
      is my God

He expresses love

And I am the recipient
   of that love;

And return it to him
   in the form
     of a
     child,

In the form of a
   painting

Or a sock that I've
   darned.

I am the mother
   of invention;

All ideas come my
   way.

I take them

Or I abort them—
   that is my
     option.

This fact has been
   too long
     hidden under
     a skirt;

Too long kept for man's
   private pleasure
   and fun.

The beauty of it
   completely
   lost—

No, just waiting
   for the right
     moment

For eyes and ears
   to hear,

God is my man
   and man
     is my God

I am Woman in
   love.

Without me
   nothing would
     exist

We have been stupid
   not to see
     this.

He has glorified me
   that I might
     glorify
     him.

And this is the time
    for recollection.

It is time for the halo
    to be restored
      to my
        head,

And tell the world
    my name too
      is God.

Because he is my
    man—

I bear his name.

Chapter IV

A CONDITIONED UNIVERSE

A CONDITIONED UNIVERSE

We were born into
   a conditioned
      universe,

Conditioned, by the mind
   to make copies of
   itself in all
      manner of
      forms and
         supportive
         inventions.

Everyday life
   is no different
      from that

Which created
   the days and
      the nights

In the beginning.

We began in those
   first days
      and nights.

We were that mind
   and are
      that mind

Of the universe,

In which we exist
   with all other
      things and
         beings.

We are individually
   and en masse
      responsible

For the conditions of
   the universe.

In the beginning
   we were not
      as we are

But as we were.

We have changed
   and grown

By meeting our
   daily needs

Individually
   and collectively.

We are unified
   because the
      mind is a
         unity

Of expression
   and receptivity—

The universe
   is a reproduction
      of this unity.

And our consciousness
        is of this
                creative process

Of the mind
        and of its
                expansion.

The universe is the
        proof of the mind's
                existence

With all of the conditions
        its own nature
                imposes.

I AM READY

To throw anything
    away that isn't
        true.

But what is Truth?

The only truth
    I know,

Is the mind itself,
    and that it
        creates all
            we call
                truth.

And can dispose
    of that

And recreate
    something new
        out of that.

So there is
    never anything
        lost

But is transfigured
    or still exits

Without any figure
    at all.

If this is not true
    there is no
        truth,

In anything I have
    written.

DEATH IS A TRANSFORMATION OF THE LIVING

And of all the conditions
    of living,

But not in a grievous
    way

For the way was set by
    ourselves,
        our interests
            and ambitions;

Our way of living
    before death.

HAVE YOU THE EYES

Have you the eyes
    to see truth

Or understand
    it is the
            mind

That provides
    the image

And sees?

CAN YOU FEEL

Can you feel
    the love
        that is

In the air,
    the friendliness

All over the universe?

I am asking myself
    and demanding
        that I do,

Because I can
    choose
        what I
            feel,

Or am conscious
    of.

WE DON'T HAVE

To depend on a
    far off God

Or winged angels
    or anything
        but

The mind.

Calling on it,
    all else
        appears,

With no time wasted

And no words wasted.

It knows even before
    we call.

It is now, more than
    ever

Trying to get our
    attention

Trying to tell us
    that it is
        us—

That it is the trees
    and the sand
        on the shore,

The buzz of the bees,

The color in the flower,

The light of the sun,

The Creator and
    the created.

We only need to comprehend
    that we are a part
        of the process—

That we are the consciousness
    the mind has produced

And that this consciousness
    is always becoming
        more alive—

More grown up
    to the creative
        process—

That it is ever active,
    ever near—

For our recognition—
    and use.

THE TWO WAVES

That Einstein perceived
  as interacting ever
    since the
      Big Bang

Act in an unchanging
  manner—

In perfect relationship
  to each other;

Thus in perfect harmony.

Never varying in act
  and reaction

They constitute
  what we have
    termed Spirit,

What we have
  termed Love,

What we have
  termed speech
    and hearing,

Sight and seeing.

This is the perfection
  we have called
    God or
      Truth.

Appearing as
  breath and
    breathing

As heartbeat
  and pulsing

As life and the
  consciousness
    of life,

As past
  and present,

As weight
  and balance,
    as ebb
      and flow,

As nuts
  and bolts,

And all of the
  two fitting
    things.

All this is the mind
  at work.

Dwelling on this
  perfection
    nurtures
      perfection

And makes things work
  smoothly for
  us.

WHAT IS LIVING

We think of it as
   being

But what was there
   before being?

The scientists say
   they can't
      imagine

A beginning—

What was there before
   the beginning?

They can't imagine
   an ending—

What would be after
   the ending?

They are thinking
   all the while
      about being.

We as beings have
   certainly evolved.

Where are we going
   if there *were* no
      beginning at the
         start?

What is meant by
   "In the beginning
      was the Word?"

It means that there
   had to be something
      which could express
      and that could perceive
         what was said,

Something to conceptualize
   its being whatever
      it is or was to
         be.

And there you have
   the basis of
      being—

Two parts of the mind
   which together
      make a
         statement.

In a word it can tell
   you what the thing
      is.

A thing has to be something
   to be called a thing.

So this is being
   but it is not
      the beginning,

Or the end—

The Word supersedes
   both.

And indicates an
      active mind.

This is what it means
      to live in
            a never

Beginning or never ending
      mind.

One that knows our
      need before
            we ask.

THIS COMES WITH SUCH EASE

It's as though I
    haven't said
        anything.

THE MIND THAT IS

Within us is our
    own personal
       God—

A God but not a
    God—

The mind that is
    universally mind
      but not
         a God

Is everywhere
    the same.

It answers a need
    wherever
        needed—

And better than
    one can imagine

Because it so
    thoroughly fills
      a space we
         have made,

Unconsciously more
    than consciously.

Consciously our mind
    is cluttered

With what we think
    we need

The universally-minded
    mind sees through

The clutter clear to
    the bottom of
      our problem

And we curse it
    more than praise

Until we see this
    mind as God
      universally

As well as our own
    personal
      God.

ALL THIS IS NOT TO

Belittle God
　　but to see how
　　　　great God
　　　　　　is

As mind,
　　how accessible, or—

How dependable.

We don't have
　　to believe

We have to know.

We don't have to
　　feel guilty
　　　　or dishonorable

Toward God.

God is all and
　　more than
　　　　we ever

Thought to be.

God is in all we
　　thought it
　　　　wasn't—

Such as, "If you make
　　your bed in hell,
　　　　there I am, also."

How?

Or who
　　has believed. . .

That God is in
　　hellish things

Or, "I am God and there
　　is none else?"

These hellish things
　　have a message
　　　　to tell.

They are an act of
　　the mind.

And mind is God

And mind is the
　　substance
　　　　of things

And all energy,
　　that substance
　　　　may have.

WE HAVE DISSECTED OURSELVES

Scientifically studying
   every function
      of sinew and
        organ,

Skeleton and bone
   and every form
      of operation.

It has been a wonderful
   age of discovery.

Even within strict
   rules and
      boundaries.

We are discovering
   how great the
      creative mind is;

Of how much ground
   it covers,

Of how impersonal

And how loving,

How brutal

And how sustaining,

How ugly and how
   beautiful.

We each choose
   how we see it
      all.

It pays no attention
   to personal
      opinion

Yet conscious
   of every thought.

It just goes on
   being itself

Creating its own
   image
      in every instance.

We can only intuitively
   know it as ourselves,

Connected with all
   of the fish,
      animals, birds,

Land and sea,
   air and
      space.

We are all together
   in this—

The starting point
   of any situation
      for change

No matter how great
   or small.

Change means evolution
    from one thing
        to another

Without losing identity
    as mind in
        action.

To depersonalize
    this mind

Would be to depersonalize
    ourselves;

So we call it God.

But to understand all
    of this

I have to see it
    in a totally
        impersonal
            way;

To lose myself in it

And take all with
    me;

To call all "we"—

As personal or as impersonal as
    we see or have
        been seeing

Ourselves.

Chapter V

IN THE FACE OF DESPERATION

IN THE FACE OF DESPERATION

Turn immediately to the
    perfection of
        mind

It will take the
    place of
        desperation

And there will be
    no more
        such a
            thing.

THE PERFECT MIND

Knows its own
    perfection.

AND MAKES ITSELF

In its own
    image.

AS CHRIST WAS DEPRIVED OF AN EARTHLY SENSE

Of father—

To realize a heavenly
    sense of
       Father,

I was deprived
    midway in years
      of an earthly
        husband

To realize the heavenly
    sense of husband.

And as Christ was crucified
    for his claims
      and vision

I will meet with
    stones of
       opposition

And criticism.

But what it all
    comes down
       to

Is that the majority
    don't realize

How good everything
    is,

And are killing each other
    off

To preserve their
    ignorance

Of a better sense
    of things.

And I must admit
    that we are all
      a little bit
        crazy—

But, oh what
    a heavenly
      craziness
       life is!

ALL OF OUR EXPERIENCES

Are due to the
    images of the
        mind

Materialized.

WE ARE SIMPLY

Images of the
    mind—

We don't have
    to bear the
        images

That we are so
    inclined
        to do.

We need to know
    when to employ
        the eraser.

I STAKE MY CLAIM

As surely as an
    old miner
        would do—

To the perfection
    of mind;

And I'll work it
    with pick
        and ax

Until I find the gold
    in my pan.

WHOLEHEARTED PRAISE

And wholehearted
    appreciation

Of the creative mind
    brings us
        perfection.

Complaints and
    dissatisfaction
        bring
            devastation.

Luckily we all
    want the
        best

So slowly we
    make
        progress.

And call it selfish
    if you
        will,

This underlying
    wanting of
        the best,

Eventually, or quickly,
    make even
        our complaints
            bring it to us.

This is why the
    scribes of old
        did write,

"Thou art a just
    and merciful
        God—"

Of the Creator of
    all things.

Now it is time
    to realize

Just how just
    and merciful
        this Creator
        is;

And know it to be
    the only mind
    there is.

TO SAY

That the mind
    is all in all

Doesn't hurt or
    manipulate
        anything.

It simply
    lets things
        be

As they should be.

There is no limit
    to this assertion's
        application.

We are talking about
    a universal
        mind;

Which creates everything
    in its own
        image.

And there is no
    other God,

Than this Creator.

It is the source
    and essence
        of everyone

And everything—

Which doesn't take
    into account anything
        but the truth.

As it knows it.

NOW SINCE THIS MIND

Is the only mind
    we have

What we claim
    as true

Will be true for us

And it will remain
    our truth until
        we change it—

By claiming something
    else

Which to the universal
    mind and to science may
        not be the
            truth at all.

The only truth
    we can
        count on is—

That the mind is
    expressive
        and receptive.

That is its creative
    nature

And that is what we
    have to work
        with.

That is what Noah
    stored in his
        ark—

"The male and female
    of every species."

And that is
    a tale

That tells us that!

With this truth
    we can drown
        everything else
        out;

Because nothing else
    is true until
        we make
        it so,

With that which
    is left.

Chapter VI

I AM AN ARMY

I AM AN ARMY

Consisting of myself
    alone.

I am here to invade
    the unknown,

To come away with
    its treasures—

The secrets it holds
    as its own.

To scatter them
    until they

Appear what they
    are—

Even to those
    who don't want
       to hear,

But shall see
    what I've
       unearthed

And am still digging
    at in order
       to share

With even those
    who are

At the bottom of the
    totem pole.

THE UNKNOWN CAN BE KNOWN

It will do us no good
    until we do
        know that

By being conscious
    of what it is
        we want to
            know,

The unknown will
    make itself
        known

In proportion to what
    we want to
        know—

And that, without
    a struggle.

It comes with
    such ease

That we deny
    its very existence

And nullify
    what we would
        otherwise
            know.

IF WE COULD REALIZE

There is only
    perfection
        in every
            thing,

We would have
    a chance

To experience
    this perfection
        in everything.

It is a matter
    of knowing
        the truth.

WE HAVE GONE THROUGH A TIME

Of being highly critical—

Of pointing out the
    things

Which irritate—

Which need to be
    scratched off
        our list
            for life.

This too, is perfect.

Can we not see
    that it is?

And free ourselves
    of the itch?

Chapter VII

INTUITIVE COMMUNICATION

INTUITIVE COMMUNICATION

Has long been generally
    out of service.

It was too open.

Boundaries were set,

Privacy desired,

Secrecy maintained
    for the elect
        and few;

Individuality developed—

Everything was divided
    into separateness.

NOW CHURCHES ARE BURNED

Boundaries invaded,

People are everywhere,

And there are no
    more locks
        or privacy.

A whole new openness
    and frankness
        abounds.

Nothing is secret anymore.

The universal mind
    is asserting
        itself.

DEEP IN OUR MEMORY

Intuition has slept—

Stored there with
    all the knowledge
        of past, present
            and future;

Built into our muscles
    and bones and
        the strands of our
            hair;

Keeping body, mind, spirit,
    and soul
        together

In one.

IMAGERY IS THE MOST

Basic way of understanding
  and the most
    basic way

The mind has of
  expressing
    itself.

Artists and poets
  particularly express themselves
    in imagery—

Through this mind
  that speaks
    in imagery—

And create the things
  they are able
    to see in
      the mind.

WE EXTERMINATE

Each other
　　like we exterminate
　　　　ants in an
　　　　　　ant hill

And years later
　　dig up their
　　　　graves

To determine
　　who is to
　　　　blame,

And who died
　　when.

How can we get out
　　of this mire?

Or should we even
　　ask that?

Just take note
　　and pass
　　　　on—

Cleansing our own
　　thoughts as
　　　　best we
　　　　　　can and to

Open the avenues
　　to better live
　　　　a good life.

CAN WE GIVE OURSELVES

Credit or discredit
    for what happens
        in the universe

If there is just
    mind?

Consciousness
    is only awareness.

Can we trust that
    the mind

Knows what it is
    doing

Beyond and below
    that which
        we are aware?

Say that of fire
    and flood,

Hurricanes and
    twisters—

Bombings, wholesale
    killings
        and such?

WHAT HAPPENS

To the consciousness
   of those whose
      bodies are blown
        to bits

In the air over the
   ocean?

Do they go on to the
   places they
      were headed
        for;

To all of the intents
   they had in
      mind?

If all is mind
   and its manifestation

Can these souls
   be unaware of
      what happened

For their protection
   and preservation?

NOW MEN ARE BOLD

Shooting legs off women
   in the street,

Bombing buildings where
   children are—

All with a straight and
   unemotional face,

Which makes us wonder,
   "Who is running
     this show?"

And how widespread
   is this attitude
     and why—

"Why?"
   We better cry.

And this question asked
   is the only good
     we can see in these
      acts.

A good, it could be,
   worth all of the sacrifice,

A universal act

A Noah's Ark flood

A higher powers act
   to show who is
     boss—

A rainbow in the
   sky, which only
     those who suffered
     most could
      see.

WHEN WE STOP AND THINK

How utterly fantastic
    this whole universe
        is,

How utterly we depend
    on it remaining
      what it is,

We think there must
    be one great
      mind

That made it all.

But stop and think—

That mind doesn't have
    to be all in
      one place.

It is everywhere;
    more perfect than if
      it were in an
        egghead
          somewhere.

It is in you and me
    and every tree,

Every squirrel and
    in the nut it eats.

Just take a look
    at the universe;

Gaze into outer
space.

It is frightening.

It seems that nothing
    we can do

Would matter a single
    bit

But just think
    bit by bit

It is all one.

Would you part
    with a single
      fingernail?

WHEN I SAY, "TURN IT OVER

To the universal
    mind,"

This wouldn't separate
    us from our
        own.

It includes concern
    for everyone
        and everything

In a conscious way
    until it becomes
        a subconscious,
            intuitive action

And brings ease
    instead of pain.

INTUITION IS A SENSE

Of connectedness with
    the mind that
        knows.

It is a sensitive form
    of the positive
        and negative.

There is something
    that is known

And a receptivity
    to that which
        is known;

A righting of or for
    interaction.

There is a feeling of
    completion
        before it is
           done.

It is our international
    telephone

Which needs no
    instrument except
        the mind.

Chapter VIII

HERE AND NOW

HERE AND NOW

I was sitting with
   a channeler
      at the table
         in my house.

I said to her, "My mother
   has been on my
      mind.

Could you contact
   her?"

She said, "Wait a minute"

And there was reflection
   and silence.

Then she asked
   with her eyes
      closed,

And in a trance,

"Was she a singer?"

And I said, with a choke,
   "yes,"
      remembering—

"Open darkened windows,
   open wide the doors,
      let a little sunshine
         in"—

In her church choir
   voice,

Sweet in the Texas
   open air.

"She is a child now
   in Italy—

She says you will
   never see
      her

But, compassion—
   the word compassion
      comes."

And I choked again
   and cried because
      we had had so many
         disagreements

About the important
   things of life;

All of which has made
   me struggle
      for years

To understand.

Then, when I could get
   my voice back

I asked, "And how about
    Tom and Sted?"

She with her eyes closed
    still, but flickering,

As though seeing things
    I had yet to see—
        hesitated,

Then flung out her hand
    and—"Sted is
        right here, you
            can ask him
                yourself."

This was too much for me
    so he told her,

"I was afraid of her
    ideas years ago."

(Afraid of my ideas!)

I never once thought
    he was afraid of
        anything.

I never thought
    of a man as
        being afraid.

And compassion
    flooded my
        mind.

"HE IS RIGHT HERE,

You can tell him
   yourself."

The impact of this
   statement

Is slowly dawning
   on me.

How often have I
   wanted through
      the years

To tell him how
   much he has
      meant to
         me.

This statement would
   indicate that
      he has been
         aware of
            my thoughts.

What a joy and relief
   it would be
      if I could know,

Not just believe,
   that he is right
      here

And I can tell him
   myself.

Christ's whole sacrifice
   was to prove

"Destroy this temple
   and in three days
      I shall raise
      it up."

Let me kick the
   melancholy

And look up
   to see the
      beauty

In that phrase
   by having that
      same consciousness,

Which doing this gives,

"Right here," now,
   embodied or not.

Embodiment
   is the product
      and form
         of thought.

If the thought is weak
   the deceased is
      only a ghost,

But I see him
   as he was,

So high—so strong—
    eyes so blue

And what he
    wore I can
        see.

How real is this?

What is the idea
    anyhow?

Christ said, "I am with
    you, always. . .

. . . I am the one at
    your door."

And I think he indicated
    that he could
        be even an animal.

I see him as the consciousness
    everywhere
        in land or sea.

And if consciousness—

It can be perceived
    by anything or anybody
        with consciousness;

Even subconsciousness,
    which makes us believe,
        or know, if you
            please.

THE SAME MIND

How can any one
   of us think
      that our
         views

Are so right and the only
   ones to have

When we all share
   the same
      mind?

We can have a
   view that
      no one else

Has yet thought
   of

But the minute
   we do

The thought is out
   there

For anyone ready
   and open
      to conceive

What it is that we
   have seen
      and
         expressed;

Or even kept to ourselves,
   supposedly,

If the mind belongs
   to the whole
      universe?

Chapter IX

I AM STRUCK DUMB

I AM STRUCK DUMB

And blind this morning
    with the realization
    of the greatness
        of the mind.

I wanted to know
    why the Bible
    fell open to
        Psalms 87

A few days ago
    when I was to
    read with
        someone

Verse 37.

We read 37
    and I pointed out
    why I wanted to
        read it to her.

But it left me wondering
    if I should
        read 87.

When I picked up the Bible
    just now

It fell open again
    of its own accord
        to Psalms 87

I was gloriously spooked
    by this presence
        of mind

That could do this to
    my dumb silence
        and blind darkness.

What am I seeing
    that I should not
        be writing about,

Or should be?

What is this and—
    why me?

Why through the ages
    has this presence
    been shrouded in
        mystery

But for a few?

And why now
    let it out?

How shall I tell
    what I have
    seen and
        heard

In a deafening and
    blinding realization

Of how great the
    mind is?

But why should it
    now remain
        in mystery?

If the mind is misused
the misuser
has to pay

That is what verse 37
has to say.

My friend was worried
about all of the
evil in the land;

Literally tearing herself
apart.

To know that the mind
is just, puts
justice in our own
hands.

And fear at our
disposal.

This shouldn't be
a mystery
anymore.

Even though it appears in strange
ways.

The thing is to know
that it will.

And to know that
this trust in it
does the job—

Of letting us know
what to do or
not to do.

Psalms 87 told me
clearly

That truth is in
my writing

Though I know not
how or why
except—

That is my desire
and intent

And that the mind is
of a mind to let
me know

How I stand.

EXCEPT FOR MY PREVIOUS

Understanding that the
    mind does not
        work willy-nilly

But in true fashion
    to its own choice

I would be in desperation
    today.

Evil doings seemed
    to be abroad
        this morning

When I awoke.

I felt it strongly in the
    air—

It had me by the
    throat—

Choking me with
    unspoken words;
    and tied up in a
        knot.

Something seemed
    afloat.

Something going
    wrong—

With a well-set plan.

Should I tackle the
    thing

And ask, "Is this really
    something,

Or what I have been
    promised and
        I myself chosen—

The real thing
    waiting in oblivion?"

This is a case of "ask no man
    but trust in the
        Lord."

And I turned back
    to what I had been
        promised

And what I had
    chosen

And fear was unleashed
    from my throat.

WHEN I PRAY

I don't have to repeat it
        for fear it isn't
                heard,

Because what I am
        praying to is the
                mind that is
                doing the
                        praying;

Mind expressing itself;

Mind receptive to what
        is expressed.

All over the universe
        mind is expressed
                and mind is heard.

And mind answers the one praying
        from wherever
                the answer is.

MIND IS THE ONE THING

We all share
    even if it is just
        a silent record
            in rocks or bones,

Or in a distant star.

This record can be
    read by those
        who know
            how.

The planet we live on
    is teaming with
        life;

Everything sharing
    the mind
        in some
            way or another.

There is even life
    within the planet

In places where the
    sun never shines.

Everything shows
    some signs
        of a mind,

Or a record that
    can be read.

To be able to read
    is a top priority

Which not everything
    has;

For words and letters.

What use has a worm
    in the ground
        for words on
        a page?

But he knows how
    to read all of
        the signs that
        he needs.

Everything has its
    own language
        for itself and
        its kind—

Its way of living—
    its creed.

Everything and its kind
    is separate from
        everything different
            from its kind.

As long as things don't
    get in each others
        way it's fine—

Until we get hungry
    for what something
        has that we don't,

Then we will have a
bite out of that.

Oh, dear, how did I get
on this?

But that is the way
   life is.

It doesn't take
   an expert
      mind reader

To figure this out—
   or to see that
      there are no limits
        of application.

Any golden rule
   or engraved tablets

Would take away
   the freedom
      of this.

The mind is universal—
   otherwise there
      would be no
        order anywhere.

But there is order,
   precision, and beauty
      everywhere;
       outside

Of our differences
   and opinions.

Surely that is where
   freedom and
      happiness is.

To see evil in the way
   we live is surely
      to die.

Is it going to take
   a complete
      catastrophe,

A complete loss
   of memory,

To free us of all of the
   sights of evil?

If dying does this

Why are we afraid
   to die?

Can we count on living
   again—where—

In this same mess?

Or in a place
   wiped clean.

This earth perhaps—

A new world for
   cleaner dreams?

Dream now
   for, yes.

In any case we will
   surely be born
      again where

We left off if not
   for this cleaning
      time.

I COULD TELL YOU

Of things that have
    happened
        to me

As strange as any
    Guru could
        tell,

But why? I have
    already said
        that the mind

Can do anything,
    say anything,
        to us

Or show us anything
    hard to believe.

Society has kept us
    within its chosen
        boundaries,

In organized control,
    in reasonable
        degrees,

Until we are ready
    and demand
        change;

In a direction demanded
    by conviction

So that just not
    anything goes.

The only reality
    is pure potentiality.

That, the mind
    has in itself

For expression
    and conception,

That we may
    tell of things
        past

And things to
    come.

SO, YES I WILL TELL

You of an experience
   I recently
      had

Because I feel
   nudged to do
      so.

One night
   when I had
      gone to
         bed

All activity within
   my body
      seemed

To have stopped,

But I was completely
   calm.

I couldn't feel
   any pulse
      in my wrist

Or hear my heart
   beat when
      I tested
         my ears.

I was keenly aware
   of my mind
      but that
         was all.

I was actually smiling
   at the experience

And got up to go to
   my studio
      to write a note
         to my son.

He had been a surgeon
   for almost
      twenty years.

But gave it up after
   a heart attack
      to give his
         full time

To being the artist
   and sculptor

He had always been.

I told him,
   "I am going back
      to bed

And going to sleep
   and just hope
      I am here

In the morning
   when I wake
      up."

I have since learned
   that others have
      through their own
      will

More advanced experiences
   such as this

And come to think of it
I have read accounts
that I dismissed from
my mind

And had forgotten about.

And when my own father
was taken to the
hospital

The Catholic sister who
felt for his pulse
quickly dropped
his wrist

And said, "How long has
this been going on?"

I shushed her, seeing that
my father hadn't
heard her
remark
with,

"Don't frighten him,"
and he died
later on that
night.

He had been put
under a see-through
tent

And everything had
been done to
keep him
alive.

But at eighty-four
and almost
completely
blind

I knew he was ready
to go.

I called my sister
in a far-off
city

And told her.

But I said, "Don't do
anything to keep
him here

Let him go
in your mind."

And when I went back
to my father
he was gone.

A few days earlier
he had quoted—

"We shall be changed. . .
. . .in a twinkling
of an eye. . .

. . . For this corruptible must
put on incorruption, and this
mortal must put on immortality. . .
. . . then shall be brought to pass
the saying that is written,
Death is swallowed up in victory."
—I Corinthians: 15, 51-54

A PRAYER AT NIGHT

Is like telling the mind
    what you want
        it

To be thinking about
    while you are asleep,

So that it doesn't make you
    do anything
        that you

Wouldn't do when
    you are fully
        conscious.

WE PRAY WITHOUT

Even knowing
   we pray

With every thought
   that we have

And the universal
   mind ripples

In a wave that
   those who are in tune
      or intuitive may
        feel.

DISTRIBUTOR OF LIFE

To this planet
    from the heavens,

Sun, moon and stars—

I can not see you
    this morning
        for the clouds

In mind or sky—
    but that is
        all right.

You are doing
    your job
        or thing.

Giving rest and moisture
    to everything

Time for groping
    through the
        dark.

Time for washing
    out the brain

To be ready for receiving
    the light of day
        when it comes—

The light of mind
    for sinew and
        bone,

For relationships
    relaxed of pain;

Washed by tear or rain.

Or just a time of
    silent waiting,

Unpushed by anything
    or thinking—

A complete mental
    clearing—

That we might be filled
    with universal will
        in the making

When the clouds
    roll by and
        the sky is
        clear.

What do the monks
    get out of
        sworn
            silence,

Broken only by
    intermittent songs
        of praise or
            supplication.

But this?

I FELT LIKE AN INDIAN

Standing in the rays
   of the early morning
      sun

And I completely understood
   their idea of the
      Great Spirit.

Though I have called
   it universal
      mind

And also called it
   two interacting
      waves,

A reverberation still
   from the first
      Big Bang

It is spirit—

The mind in action!

And I see all life,
   all consciousness,
      all creative invention
         depending on it.

There would be nothing
   but for this
      Great Spirit—

This great universal
   spirit.

This is what, be it Indian,
   white man, yellow
      or black,
         we praise.

It would be great
   if we could drop
      all other differing
      ideas

Of what it is and
   just worship
      the bare nakedness
      of this;

One idea that is at the
   base of all ideas
      and religions

And feel this spirit
   enveloping
      and activating
      us all—

In all common
   cause.

After that and not
   forgetting that

We could put on all
   our ornamented
      headdresses,

Pick up the drums,

Put on our robe embroidered
   in gold,

Light candles to it
   or twig flares
      without feeling this way,
        or our way

Of honoring this Great Spirit
   is the only way.

And we could enjoy
   and enter into the spirit
      of all pageantry

In the name of
   the Great Spirit—

In native art and
   cultures everywhere.

And in all of nature's
   animal, bird,
      bug, or worm's
        lives.

They all have their way
   of living and
      enjoying life.

We all have this one thing
   in common,

A consciousness!

A spirit!

The one and only thing
   that we can
      call life.

I HAVE MADE

A huge discovery,

That others regard me
        with the same
                regard I have
                        for them.

Not in exact words
        or in the same
                detail

Like black and
        white

So that it can be
        plainly seen,

But in a complete
        maze of
                disguised
                        array.

I've been dazed
        and completely
                lost in all
                        of this

For days and months
        and years.

Finally giving up,

It all dropped away
        as though it
                had never been,
                        or happened.

And then and now
        I see the true
                them and
                        me.

Chapter X

I WAS ALONE

I WAS ALONE

In my thinking
    in 1947

When I wrote my
    first poem.

It came to me in the
    night to meet
        my desperation

For knowledge.

Now after all this time
    the whole world
        is catching up
            with me.

It is time to move on
    in the area that
        all this knowledge

Has been leading me
    to.

There have been people
    before me

There always have been,
    but with only
        a hint or two

Of what I wanted to
    know.

And that is what is
    true for me
        now.

There are hints and
    suggestions about
        life after death

And a lot of dream-like
    speculation.

I want to know the
    truth if there
        is yet such a
    thing as
        truth.

All that we can
    attain is experience,

And that has to be
    weighed and
        measured

In the collection
    of experience
        others have
            had.

So, I am calling in
    a hypnotist

To look, or help me
    to look, into
        areas of life

Which I have closed
    a lid on,

As not being relevant at
    the time,

So that I could get on
    with the then
        present.

This is not a new idea
    as I have said
        before.

The hypnotist I am calling in,
    is a doctor of this
        science.

But it will be new
    for me

And I'll expect
    that I will have
        something to
            add to it,

Because this is the
    way that
        knowledge
            moves forward.

The thought that
    we know it
        all consciously

Is all wrong.

The mind is expanding.

The truth is always
    further out
        there.

Dogma is the trouble
    with organized
        religions

We should never stop
    there with
        either one of them;

Neither should we
    abandon,

But leave them for
    what they are—

Just stepping stones—
    and walk
        on,

Laying down more
    stepping stones
        as we go
            along.

Time ahead could be
    looked at in
        this regard.

And that is what
    I am doing.

For the sake of myself
    and for others
        if they chose to

Accept anything from
    it,
        for their own.

I WAS TO HAVE

My first session
   with the hypnotist
      on this day.

I woke in the night
   and though I had
      long been awaiting
         this occasion,

I was asking myself,
   "what is it that I
      want to know?"

I felt unexcited and confused,

I wrestled with this
   for hours.

I felt as Jacob must
   have felt—

His head on a rock
   for a pillow
      and all alone
         on strange ground.

He wrestled with an
   angel, it was
      said,

Whose name he did
   not know.

"What is your name?" he
   asked and he
      said, "I will not
         let you go until
            you bless me."

And it was almost
   dawn for him and almost
      dawn for me
         before I knew.

But I did know
   and felt blessed.

I wanted to know
   about a passage
   I had made—
      not about details of
      ordinary days
         of the past, but

How did I make
   a transition—

And what was there
   in making it.

And what brought me
   from there to
      this?

I WAS TOO ALERT

For the hypnosis
    to work.

I was trying too hard
    to understand
        the whole thing.

I couldn't relax and
    go to sleep
        to give the idea

Time to sprout.

I was constantly
    digging it up
        in my mind,

While it was still
    just a seed.

The woman has to
    sleep with
        her man.

One has to give
    the non-stuff
        of all stuff

A chance to take form
    without interference;

A gestation period.

This is what I think
    hypnosis is
        about.

A time to reshape
    a memory of
        incident or
        image

Which has had a
    long time or a
        short time

Of sleep.

A time of being nothing
    but memory or
        plan.

But that complete,
    which we can
        count on if to be
        a child

Of having ten fingers
    and ten toes,

When it comes.

Or the full picture
    of an engine
        which has never
        been made,

If that is what has
    been in the gestation
        period.

THE GARDEN OF EDEN

Is a frame of mind
  in complete
    trust in itself.

It doesn't see itself
  as two which
    could be
      parted

But as one
  in complete
    companionship

Of that which Is
  and that which
    could be.

If one doesn't see
  this

They, or he or she,
  are out of harmony—

Out of Eden.

And have to struggle
  hard, believing
    they are

All by themselves—

They sweat and plow
  and turn over
    the ground.

They look in every
  direction

Except the right
  one—

To themselves!

Where that which Is
  and that which
    could be are
      one—

A perfect hologram,

Which no matter
  how many times
    you slice it

These two are there
  eternal in the
    heavens—

Supply and demand—

Available in
  self-trust.

Which means
  a trust which

Universally applies
  to everyone.

And also means
    as long as the
        universal mind
          is what it
            is,

As one that speaks
    for itself.

WHEN I WENT OUT THIS MORNING

To walk with my
    little dog,

To breathe the freshness
    of the air,

To feel the warmth
    of the sun
        on eyelids,

The solid earth
    beneath my
        feet;

I turned back knowing
    that I could leave
        every cell, organ, skin
          and bone;

Every thought to the order
    of it all.

So what responsibility
    do I have?

Is all but, "vanity, vanity
    everywhere?"

Are we any better off
    than the animals?

I could live with
    much, much
        less.

All my life I have
    been driven
        by a sense

Of creativity, but
    today I feel
        completely relaxed.

So why am I
    writing?

I'll tell you why—

There would never have been
    anything but
        for a sense of
          creativity;

A sense of wonder
    and a spark
        of love

To be expressed.

THE CREATIVE MIND

Works like the nuts
    and bolts of
        machinery.

If you have a bolt,
    or a drawer full
        of bolts,

But you can't find
    a nut that will
        take it,

You're out of luck.

If you have a good
    idea

But you can't come
    up with the feeling
        that it will work

You are out of luck.

Or how about this—

When Christ was asked
    to do a healing

He would sometimes say
    "Believest thou that
        I can do this?"

The female part of the
    mind has to do
        its part

Of fully conceiving
    your idea.

No wishy-washy halfway
    believing.

No complete abortion
    of the idea
        will do—

No backing away
    in any excuse;

The two parts of the mind
    have to be in
        complete companionship

In other words—

In Love!

This is why we can
    say—

God is love.

But don't forget,
    it takes two to
        make love.

And don't forget
    Genesis 1: 26 & 27
        "Let us make man
        in our image. . .
            . . . male and female
            created he *them* ."

119

BUT HERE IS ANOTHER WAY

Of looking at the
   workings of the
      mind.

If there is an ill fit
   just like the nuts
      and bolts idea,

You have the perfect
   right and option
      without question

To not try to make
   it fit.

Even in an unwanted
   pregnancy.

But that is much
   harder to put down
      than an ill-fitting
         nut for a bolt.

So this calls for a lot
   of predetermination
   to not just pick
      up any old thing
      and try to make
      it work.

This calls for a solid
   philosophy and for
      knowledge of

Just how the mind
   works.

Even so we learn
   by our own mistakes
      if not before.

The thing to do is to
   make the most
      of life;

And you can do
   and I can too

For life is malleable only
   to its own
      making.

DEAR CRESCENT MOON

Have you any idea
    how beautiful
        you are;

Low in the western sky
    and snow on the
        ground this January
            night;

As I look at you
    from my warm
        house

Through tops of
    bare cottonwood
        trees, asleep

Beside the river
    below?

THE LAST TIME I EVER

Punished a son
    I punished both of them
        together

For fighting—

And I threw myself down
    on the bed between
        them

And bawled.

I could cry myself sick
    even today

For things that were
    said to each other
        or to me that hurt.

But when my oldest
    drew his last breath
        at fifty-seven,

The cry that went from
    my lips was,
        "my baby!"

Most of our life
    together was
        pure fun

So why do I remember
    a single incident
        or two.

I think we need these
    few to bring us
        to

Compassion.

To a sense of
    unconditional
        love.

A love where
    no set conditions
        remain.

It takes a strong person
    to reach this aim

But there will be no
    peace in the world
        until it happens.

I WALKED THIS MORNING

Over the path
    that Sted's feet
      trod.

Once he told me,
    "I had no pain

And I knew it was
    because of you.

I wish I knew
    what you were
      doing,

But you just can't
    teach old dogs
      new tricks.

I know that my trouble
    is largely because
      of this—

And I wish that I
    could understand—

But I simply can't,
    Myrtle."

My heart aches for
    him still.

And I have to know
    if his soul
      still lives

And how!

He is always in my
    mind.

Is that a sign
    that he still
      is—

Or am I just kidding
    myself?

I have to know
    the solution,

Not just some
    fairy tale.

I want a real rapport
    with him,

All life and nature
    is so beautiful
      and perfect

It stands to reason
    that it couldn't
      bring us this far

And cut us off.

There shouldn't be
    anything standing
    in our way

Of seeing a future.

Even he said, "We will
   be together again,"

An unbeliever of what
   he was taught
      as a child.

Had to believe what
   he said,

Or he wouldn't have
   said it.

He was honest with himself
   and with me.

I too was taught a lot
   of nonsense

With only an inkling
   of truth,

When I was a child.

But this inkling
   is worth

All of the nonsense
   I am having to
      wade through.

And this is what
   he also
      sensed,

To be waiting in the
   offing for
      him.

STED HOW COULD

I love you still
   if you don't
      exist?

I think of you as
   you used
      to be

But what were you
   then and
      what

Now?

In living terms—

This can not go on
   as before.

As you are no more
   to be seen;
      yet are.

The word "living" has to
   be redefined

To include all the things
   that come to
      mind.

Such as music heard
   by the one who
      can write
         it.

Paintings to be painted
   as visualized.

Houses to be built
   as we work them
      out on paper,

Roads to be built
   and pathways
      to continents,

And ways to get to
   other planets.

This is what is meant
   by "Let us make
      man in our
         image,"

In the image the mind
   has of him.

We can not imagine anything
   we do not understand
      first, in some way.

Comprehension has to
   stop dragging
      its feet

On this issue
   and produce
      results;

But it is the woman
   in labor

And she will give us
   a newborn
      consciousness

Of what life really
   is.

This woman is the woman
   in all of us

We are not just men,
   or man as we
      are spoken of.

Or human as apart
   from Divine

Or man apart from
   all nature.

We are the living mind
   alive in every
      thing,

And it has to be both
   male and female

Which is to say
   expressive and
      receptive.

This is where life is
   and what it is—

Mind in action.

You can call it Spirit
   if you want to,
      or Love,

What difference does it
   make—

Nothing to be fighting
   over!

Differences of opinion
   doesn't change
      the mind's
         nature.

To understand this,
   would be the healing
      of the leaves
         of the little book

The angel in Revelation
   has to offer in
      its hand.

STED, I WOKE THIS MORNING

So utterly lonely
    for the feel of
        your touch,

But after a while
    I heard your
        voice

Come to me from
    the past.

"Don't think," you said,
    and I relaxed,

And you cupped my
    face with
        your hands.

I OFTEN THINK

That I might have
    had a past
        high in the
            mountains

In a one room cabin
    with stove, table,
        chair and a bed,
            two small windows
                and a heavy
                    door—

With nothing but
    the landscape
        below,

And a village.

In my cabin I lived as a sage,
    an ageless woman,

Companioned by thought
    and memory alone.

And I look at what
    I have now—

It is the same
    only in a different
        age

Where young people
    come

And find a different world
    than their
        own,

And breathe the sweetness
    of the air—

Read my books
    and go
        home.

I no longer paint
    or build houses

I don't have to do
    a thing
        but think,

Or just be.

It is a golden
    precious
        time
            for me.

A time others long for—

An effortless time.

MY HOUSE

Has the same
    flavor of
        that long ago
           cabin,

With little more
    than a bed,
        a table, a chair,
           and a stove

With a hundred years
    or so of invention

And I have
    slightly
        changed,

But the same

Little old lady
    with thought a
        little more
             grown up—

To fit the day
    and age

And to fit the
    future beyond.

The young still come
    and sit by
        my fire.

I HAVE NO SUPERFLUOUS

Flowers, no fancy
   tricks about
      the place;

Its beauty is simplicity
   itself in a
      big way,

Inside and out.

There is just open land
   and trees in a
      stand,

Along the river
   where they are
      happy to be,

Without any care
   from me.

Immediately around
   the house the
      grass is
         mowed;

Not in a straight line
   but in a curve
      and a swirl.

A bird feeder on a
   post just outside
      a large window

Before which I and
   friends sit
      is of great interest.

Along with an open field,
   and mountains
      beyond;

Cut in two with a highway
   where cars and
      trucks, bicycles
         and joggers
      belong.

A television in a room
   also keeps me
      posted on what
         is going on.

Otherwise I can look
   over the heads
      of passersby

And cut off the television
   with the push of a
      button

And live in my own
   quiet meditation

On how things in the
   past have been

And what is now
   or is to come.

WHEN I THINK AND WONDER

About *Things To Come*
   I am not thinking
      of a new car
         or house;

I am thinking about
     things that matter
        to me.

At age eighty-eight
     going on eighty-nine
        then ninety,

I don't need a motorcycle
   or the things
      young people
        do.

They are living in
   the now as
      I did when I
        was young.

I want to know—

Will I have any more
   birthdays coming
      after I am
        gone?

Chapter XI

I AWOKE THIS MORNING

I AWOKE THIS MORNING

With a creative sense
    of expectancy—

A beautiful feeling
    felt in every cell—

What can I say of this
    that will quicken
        and touch everyone
            on the planet?

It is a stirring of life
    that everyone
        shares

Especially for those
    who have been
        depressed.

Depression makes
    a great hole

That cannot but be
    filled, at last
        to overrunning

With this awakening
    feeling of expectancy.

And I cry, "Oh God,
    thank you
        for this

Saving grace."

This basic thing—

This way of the creative
    mind that
        is so big

That it accounts
    for the whole
        universe

And every mite
    within it.

This is the great
    male and female
        in whose image
            we are made—

To feel what they,
    as of one mind
        feel—

To
    Bear and give birth
        to feelings.

Instinctively, we have
    to do this
        and live;

To create as we
    are created—
        whatever it is

That we want to create—
    barrel, shovel
        or steel.

Relax, for it is a gift
     just, "Let there be,"

For it already is
     in your mind

When you think
     of it;

Then give of yourself
     as we are given
          and see it
               materialize.

THE ENERGY OF THE UNIVERSE

Is the universal mind
   in action.

There is no mind
   apart from this
      mind;

No energy from
   anything
      but this mind.

The twists and turns
   the floods and
      storms,

Yes and no,
   the wars,
      the bombs,

The births and abortions
   are all the actions
      of mind.

There is no judgment,
   no morals
      involved.

The mind simply
   acts unconditionally

For there is no good
   or evil in
      the mind.

Consciousness is the
   consciousness of this
      mind of itself.

There is no logical
   accounting for
      a mess.

The mind remembers
   everything and
      is continuously
         adding to—

Or illuminating—

By changing it to
   something
      else;

Another name
   or food for game,

Nothing lost.

A shot of adrenaline for
   the pain,

Or light at the end
   of the tunnel.

There is magic in its
   every action,
      because we don't
         know it, still—

It doesn't know itself
    what it will do next.

The mind is pure
    potential;

The stuff our dreams
    are made
        of.

And the only reality
    of things.

IF THERE ARE NO MORALS

That control the mind
    what is there?

The answer is universal
    order.

With no thought, "Is it
    good or bad?"

What does the Bible say,
    oh yes,
        "In the day that ye
        shall know both
            good and evil
            ye shall die."

I think it says, "surely die."

So we must be on the
    wrong track.

But I know that it
    is not because
        we are naked

And have sex.

To think this way has been
    our downfall.

To think anything bad
    that the mind
        makes is—
            bad itself.

"As a man thinketh, so
    is he," is the
        universal order
            of the day.

We need to back up
    and start all over
        again.

No moral prejudice allowed
    or even considered.

We need to be stripped
    of all unnecessary
        trappings

To know what nakedness
    means.

It means that the mind
    is nothing but
        the creator and the
            created—

No other power
    involved!

THE SCIENTISTS TELL US

That all of our body
    parts are renewed
        within a year;

That cells die
    and are sloughed
        off

And new ones appear.

Then what is it that
    grows old?

Wrinkles, they say
    come about
        by how

We use our face—

Creasing it in smiles

Or creasing it in frowns.

Then it is how we
    hold on to memory

That renew the
    wrinkles and
        scars

In tissue and bone.

Our greatest fear
    is death or
        loss of memory.

Often, we are told, there
    is a complete
        rewind

Of our whole life
    experience,
        in the

Greatest of detail,
    just before
        death.

What happens to that
    tape,

That rewind of memory?

Is it edited or played
    again as is—

In a new body, born.

Or how about that
    new body each
        year?

Why not edit it
    as we go along
        from day to
            day.

This, I am sure, we
    do without even
        thinking about
            it.

But what if we
   knew about
      it?

And made a concerted
   effort—

A conscious knowledge
   that we can
      erase the errors we

Make up as we go
   along.

This we do, I am
   convinced

In criticism and
   wars.

But unconsciously
   on our own part

We are making
   history

And see what we
   have done in
      a hindsight
         view

Of things.

Thus we come along
   and evolve
      in spite of ourselves,

Because there is always
   the future
      ahead.

MAGGIE—

That scare you had
    that your first
        pregnancy

Was not all right
    could have been
        that little
          girl

You were—

Neglected by your
    dad.

It just had to know
    that it was
        wanted

Before it came
    into the world.

Your pregnancy
    came as a
        surprise

"That little monster
    within me!"
        you cried.

But when really
    questioned,

"Do you want me
    or no?"

You really had
    to make up
        your
          mind.

Much soul searching
    was done

And other opinions
    and desires
        put aside

You alone had to
    decide.

The answer was,
    "yes—yes
        no matter what, I
    am keeping
You!"

That made the baby's image
    by sonar sound
        appear all right—

Baby and mother to be
    of one
        mind

As was universally
    designed to
        be—

And it *is* a girl,
    with all the
        promise

Of perfect child,
    who had decided
        itself

That it wanted
    to come,

Father-daughter wound
    healed

In mother-daughter
    episode,

Instead of being
    carried over into
        another generation,

If that is the way
    genes
        work—

In mental determination
    on their own.

THE PERFECT POTENTIAL

Is our rock of Gibraltar—

It is mind free
    of judgment,
        free of strain;

A perfect relaxed
    state of being

Completely in the
    arms of love;

Completely submissive
    and ready to
        conceive a

Whole new idea
    to be born

Whose birthing
    could bring universal
        joy.

This is what all advancement,
    all scientific work,
        all effort in the art
            of living
                is about.

This only comes
    when all else
        has been to no
            avail.

At a time
    when the struggle
        has been too
            much

And against all
    odds.

But there it is

Just where you thought
    it was not.

MIND IS GOD AND THERE IS NONE OTHER

Everything falls under
    that statement—

Everything is a form
    of the mind.

Nothing can claim
    to be equal
        or to have
            precedence.

Every function
    is a function
        of the mind.

All presence is the
    presence of the
        mind.

Nothing can claim
    to be equal
        in the sense

Of being other.

There should be no
    question of
        being other

When all is mind.

What more could we
    want than
        that which
            is?

And all?

WHAT GIVES THE HEART ACTIVITY?

If—

Believing that the heart
    takes precedence
        over the mind

Just ask yourself

How could the heart
    act at all
        but for the fact

That the mind is what
    is giving it its
        activity—

And what is its substance
    but mind in the
        form of heart?

We keep repeating
    mistaken ideas

When we don't see
    this basic structure
        of the totality of
            everything.

Lacking this basic idea
    we split hairs
        dissect ourselves
            confuse the issue

And fall short
    of the beauty
        of simplicity

And lack the harmony
    that is

Running everything
    in spite of our
        lack of understanding.

Only by being receptive
    to the truth of the
        mind's expressiveness

Can we realize that
    in our receptiveness

We are one with its
    expressiveness

And are not just a product
    of the mind,

But are one with
    its creativity.

We are no longer
    just conscious
        of the mind

But are the receptive
    side, equal
        to its expressiveness

And a partner in equal
    status

And no longer just
      observing the
           mind

But are in full-grown
      operation in its
           creativity.

We no longer need
      to depend on
           guides

Or wonder where
      the Gods of old
           hide.

Chuck it all
      because you
           are it

With all that is.

WHEN I SAY

We have no need
    for guides,

I mean they are
    everywhere—

Guideposts
    personal or
        impersonal,

Good or bad
    pointing the
        way to carry
          out

Our intent—
    whatever that
      is.

SINCE WE ALL HAVE TO GO

Don't you think we
    should know
       where we
          are going?

Who should know
    but those who have
      already gone?

"Take no thought of
    thine own self, but
       trust in the Lord."

Like going to sleep
    at night trusting
      that we will be here
        when we wake
         up.

Is that why we don't
    know where we
      are going?

Will we be right here
    just like waking
      up?

It's got to be something
    as crazy as that.

But who can tell us
    with our ears
      plugged up?

We should know
    but, why don't we?

Who can show us
    with our eyes
      shut?

I want to see
    and hear from
      the ones who have
        been there;

That is a must,

And I feel that it is
    up to me.

If it is a fact
    I should be able
      to know
        it

If I could just
    wake up.

And I probably will
    without any effort
      on my part.

What a relief it must
    be to have no thought
    or "take no thought
      for thine own self—
      but trust in the Lord."

My mother had this
    trust

And it used to annoy
    me.

I wanted to know
    for sure.

The church-going people
    don't need to be
        worried about me;

This is the way I want it.

I want to find out for
    myself.

I HAD A DREAM

I saw a little girl.

I thought it was myself
    born again in Italy.

I was on my mother's
    arm

A little chemise on
    one side partly
        fallen off my
            shoulder.

There was a knowing
    smile on the little
        girl's face, in profile.

I took a finger
    and lifted the
        chemise
            back

On her shoulder.

I received a note
    with a picture
        on the front

Of a grown lady
    with the same
        profile

And the same knowing
    smile,

A psychic, no less

I pondered and kept
    it for awhile.

Then one day through
    a channeler
        (as I have already said)

My mother told me
    that she was a little
        girl in Italy;

That I would never
    see her but,

"Compassion." she said

And I took it for
    myself.

Someday we will
    look back from
        the year 2000

And maybe long for
    what we now
        think of as boredom.

I CAN SEE DYING

As a means of cleansing
    the spirit so
        to speak.

If we see spirit
    as the act of
        pure mind,

Just life at its
    purest;

Then we can see that
    memory of hatred,
        false beliefs,
            errors of thinking,

Are hidden or lost,

And the spirit (the activity
    of the mind)

Is all that remains
    to begin again

In a pattern more
    benign;

A pattern designed to live
    having no death
        penalty built in.

I can see—with the way
    things are at this time—

That we have a lot of
    dying to do.

WE ONLY DIE

To live again,
   to take care
      of unfinished
         business.

I have a friend
   who is in hospital,

Waiting for doctors
   to find the trouble;

She is just sitting
   and waiting
      while wasting
         away.

In this time of waiting
   what is she
      thinking
         about?

I love her dearly
   but what can
      I do?

I know we all
   have a part
      to play

With family and
   friends.

A silent one

One of releasing them
   of criticism or
      expressing praise.

This is a healing
   for self
      or friend.

For now
   or then.

When born again,
   or going
      home,

To make amends
   prompted by
      some mental
         nudging,

Without a word,
   from family
      or friends

Even needed.

STED MATERIALIZED

Before me in a
   dream

And I told him, "Sted,

I never thought I would
   ever see you
      looking at me
         this way."

I saw approval and
   pride and
      joy

To see me, in his
   face

And the way he
   came before
      me;

As though today
   and all the
      time in
         between
            were

In my mind exactly
   as they were
      and are.

And here he
   was

Materialized in
   a dream.

ANOTHER TIME

Recently Sted appeared
    before me

And gave me a
    great big
        hug,

Then people on a
    rooftop called
        to him,

"Are you coming?"
    and he was
        gone;

Brief moment of
    joy to last
        forever
            mine.

WE HAVE A MIND

That can free us
     from all restrictions
          and restraint

But think of what
     chaos that
          could bring.

Until we get over
     the idea that
          chaos is fun

And exciting
     we better stick
          to the plow.

ALL OBJECTIVITY

Is a dream
    materialized.

All is mind and
    the forms
        of mind.

There are no limits
    to its possibilities

In daily life
    or all eternity.

When we put our foot
    in a boat

We could be immediately
    on the other shore

But for doubt.

This calls for topsy-turvy
    in our believing.

So let us go back
    to Eden now.

Why were we there
    subjected to the
        plow?

Why fallen to earth
    to seem molded
        of this clay

Or see the woman
    made second
        to man?

This is but a dream
    that needs to be
        vaporized!

Man is not fallen;

He stands upright

And the woman walks
    not behind him,

But by his side

He is light,

She is darkness.

This is the image
    made of God.

No objectivity
    could be, but
        for this.

The story of Mother Earth
    or Mother Church
        is but a farce.

She is no less
    than the half
        of God.

He could not be Father
　but for her!

And the son is heir
　to both.

It is time this
　daughter should
　　be born.

This bride-to-be
　of the Christ

To put objectivity
　in its rightful
　　place—

A dream conceived
　and fulfilled
　　by her—

On earth
　but not of it.

It is of him and her,
　in heaven and
　　earth.

This brings us back
　to why we
　　say,

Mother Earth and
　Mother Church

For like the Father and
　with the Father
　　She is everywhere

And in everything,

Objectivity

In the making—
　and the made.

STANDING IN THE SUN

With my little
   black dog
      this morning

I asked, "what do you
   have to say to me?"

All I got was, "Be still
   and know that
      I am God."

All was still—

Not a leaf was stirring,

Not a cloud was moving
   in the sky.

Every flower was turned
   toward the sun
      waiting.

I looked about me
   and all was
      still.

Every leaf and twig
   held a wetness
      from a nightly
         rain

Which came without
   a flash of light
      or thunder;

It just fell

And everything was
   still.

It is a time for
   taking it all
      in for

Further action.

I took a deep breath
   and returned
      to my pen

And it silently
   records my
      thoughts;

And my dog to
   takes her place
      watching.

THE SCIENTISTS

Do well to say
    that it would
        take an
           artist,

Or a poet to tell us
    how the first life
        on the planet

Came about from
    something of the
        stuff of the
           universe

Knowing how to make
    copies of
        themselves.

The scientists see the
    facts of existing
        things.

Their drive for fact
    have made them
        overcome stupendous
        odds.

And always will
    until we know
        far more about
        the universe

Than we know, the why
    that gave the stuff
        drive.

The creative urge is what
    art and poetry
        are about.

The scientists see no
    God or gods out
        there

Because it or they
    are unseeable

And escape the most
    powerful
        microscope.

They or it do not
    seeably
        seem to
           exist,

But are before
    the fact

And do show existence
    in the transformation
        to fact.

They are the fact
    and the idea
        before the fact

As art and poetry
    both
        are.

AND I WILL LEAVE YOU

With this mind-boggling
   thought

That mind is
   timeless,

Presence
   leading us
      into all

Things to come
   whatever.

Maybe it took
   the "Big Bang"

Or the "explosive
   declaration"

To make us become
   prepared to make
      copies of ourselves.

And the cause of our
   becoming conscious.

Our planet is just
   a speck in the universe

But how can we be
   the only ones having
      a consciousness?

The universe is
   expanding;

The explosive
   declaration
      has sent our
        wits in

Every direction.

And it has been
   pleasant
      and exciting.

We can't imagine a
   future time of
      collapsing

Nor should we,
   except to realize
      how fortunate
        we are to
         be

Expanding.

And that collapsing
   will be of that
      same

Potential, waiting
   for us in the
      wings.

CONSCIOUSNESS

Cannot by definition
    be unconsciousness

So herein is life
    eternal.

There is nothing
    to die

There was nothing
    but the mind
        in the first
            place

Conscious of
    itself.

There is not then
    a trinity

As though something
    other than
        a copy

Of that which
    we could
        not otherwise
            see.

Death then is "swallowed
    up in victory. . .

. . . in a twinkling
    of an eye. . . "

www.ingramcontent.com/pod-product-compliance
Lightning Source LLC
Chambersburg PA
CBHW022009080426
42733CB00007B/538